At the Police Station

by Diana Noonan
illustrated by Christina Booth

SCHOOL PUBLISHERS

Printed in China

ISBN 10: 0-15-350408-0
ISBN 13: 978-0-15-350408-2

Ordering Options
ISBN 10: 0-15-350332-7 (Grade 2 Below-Level Collection)
ISBN 13: 978-0-15-350332-0 (Grade 2 Below-Level Collection)
ISBN 10: 0-15-357435-6 (package of 5)
ISBN 13: 978-0-15-357435-1 (package of 5)

11 12 13 14 15   0940   15 14 13 12 11 10

Characters

Reporter 1

Reporter 2

Dispatcher

Officer 1

Officer 2

Setting: A police station

Reporter 1: Here we are at the police station. Let's talk to Officer Snow.

Reporter 2: What is your job, Officer Snow?

Dispatcher: I am a police dispatcher. I answer calls for help.

Reporter 1: There is a call right now.

Dispatcher: Hello? This is the police call center. What is the problem? Where is it?

Reporter 2: The dispatcher tells the officers where they are needed. She radios them in their car.

Dispatcher: Officers! You are needed at High Street.

Officer 1: What is going on?

Reporter 1: Officer Snow tells the officers the facts.

Dispatcher: I just got a call.

Officer 2: What did you learn?

Dispatcher: The traffic lights on High Street are broken. Cars are everywhere.

Officer 1: Are there any other facts?

Reporter 2: The dispatcher makes sure the officers have a good idea of the problem.

Dispatcher: There are many angry drivers on High Street. One driver hit another car and then drove away. No one was hurt though. That driver must be caught!

Officer 1: We're on our way!

Officer 2: Let's go!

Reporter 1: The officers keep in touch with the station using their radio.

Dispatcher: I try to help the officers.

Reporter 2: A police station is a busy place!

Think Critically

1. What did you think would happen when you read that the traffic lights were broken on High Street? Why?

2. How did the police officers find out about the accident? What did they do?

3. What was the Dispatcher's job?

4. What tells you that this story is a Readers' Theater?

5. If you could be a character in the Readers' Theater, who would you be? Why?

 **Social Studies**

Write a Paragraph Write a paragraph telling why police officers are important and how they keep the community safe.

School-Home Connection Tell a family member about the story. Then talk about why road safety is important.